With heart, soul and voice

100 years of the Manx Music Festival

by

Martin Faragher

Leading Edge ™
press and publishing
in association with
THE MANX MUSIC FESTIVAL

The title of this book is a phrase from the Manx national anthem, which was first sung at the 1907 Manx Music Festival and dedicated to Lady Raglan. She and Lord Raglan, Governor of the Isle of Man, were enthusiastic supporters of this festival.

Walter Gill, who wrote the words, stated that he had adapted the Manx folk song *Mylecharane* into "more singable form, a gracious and lovable tune that can never die" and he merely hoped that it would "stand side by side, although at a respectful distance from God Save the King". It was disparaged as "the banal little ditty that has been foisted upon the Manx people as their National Anthem" but its singing by the assembled thousands at their national music festival led to its acceptance. *Then let us rejoice with heart soul and voice* is still sung there, but no longer side by side with that other national anthem.

The cover is based on a motif used early this century in the festival programme.

Published by Leading Edge Press & Publishing Ltd, The Old Chapel, Burtersett,
North Yorkshire, DL8 3PB. ☎ (0969) 667566 in association with The Manx Music Festival

A CIP Catalogue record for this book is available from the British Library

ISBN 0-948135-32-8

Design by Barbara Allen
Cover design by Ruth Abbott
Type by Leading Edge Press & Publishing Ltd
Printed and bound in Great Britain by Ebenezer Baylis & Son Ltd, Worcester

Contents

Acknowledgements

The Manx Music Festival, better known as the Guild, has shaped and reflected the cultural and social life and even the national aspirations of a small but distinctively independent Island community.

There is always something more waiting to be found out for a book like this, and my four years of research had to be curtailed as the festival's centenary drew near. I had already given a paper on its early years which is inVol X no 1 of the Proceedings of the IoM Natural History and Antiquarian Society. The main source of information has been printed ephemera and the few surviving old minute books, and for access to these thanks are due to the patient staff of the Manx Museum Library, and to Joan Hinnigan, the secretary of the Manx Music Festival.

Two previous secretaries, Edith Gallagher and Pamela Duchars, have also helped, while many others have furnished more reminiscences and photographs than could be used. However the sole responsibility for accuracy, opinions and conclusions is mine, and if I have omitted the very thing in which some reader takes pride, this has not been done out of prejudice.

Finally, I wish to thank the committee of the Manx Music Festival and its chairman Noel Cringle MHK, and the Isle of Man Bank which has assisted them with the cost of production, for making possible the book which Margaret Faragher would have loved to see. It has been a labour of love.

Martin Faragher, 1991

Chapter 1

1892-1918:
The rise of a musical nation

It was in December 1892 that the fifth Annual Exhibition of the Isle of Man Fine Art and Industrial Guild first included music. This Guild did not survive the Great War but it is still the name by which the Manx Music Festival is better known.

A local paper had announced the forthcoming novelty at the 1892 Exhibition: "This year one or two new features have been introduced which will make the Guild more attractive and interesting, notably exhibitions of fishing nets, jewellery boots and shoes... Then there are the choir competitions arranged by Miss Wood, also a new and instructive feature, which have aroused much interest; and the school work cannot fail to be productive of many beneficial results among the young, while fostering a spirit of healthy rivalry which is certain to have good effect."

The people who sang or listened on that December day could not have known that those six music competitions would soon grow into a fervent assembly of thousands, with great choral works performed under famous conductors and the Manx language and folk music was kept alive.

Of course it is no longer true what the papers said in 1921: that the big night of the Manx Music Festival is one of the two occasions in the year when any Manx person can count on seeing almost any other Manx person. But then that is no longer true of Tynwald Fair, the annual meeting of the Manx legislature, which was the other occasion referred to. Nevertheless this festival has survived as the event which fosters, not only musicians almost from the cradle (and not long ago an under-four did sing), but also

music critics almost to the grave.

For this to have happened however, more ordinary people had to have time and money to spare, and more musical education, than hitherto. In 1892 the visiting industry was still rapidly expanding, drawing people from the country to provide board and lodgings for the the holiday-makers, together with such back-up services as baking, brewing, building and banking.

The intensive seasonal nature of the visiting industry meant that most leisure activities had to be in the winter. Moreover tourism involved a high proportion of women, and those who were actually in business had a high degree of social and financial independence. It was also a time when church and chapel were the centre of social life, so that from an early age people sang praises to the Lord, and often discovered that He had given them a good voice at no cost. Such factors influenced the nature of the Manx Music Festival and so it has always provided "something to do in the winter".

The growth of music-making

In the later years of the nineteenth century, communal music-making was an everyday part of life, not only at church and school and civic occasions but also in the public houses and music halls.

From 1863 Curwen's Tonic Sol Fa method had been popularised as a means for singers to read music, and it had its own training college, magazine and music-publishing house. With the rise of compulsory schooling (from 1872 in the Isle of Man), this system was eagerly adopted by the teachers, many of whom were products of church training colleges where choral worship was a daily event.

It was around 1860 that Oxford and Cambridge universities instituted systematic degrees in music, so that its study became academically respectable. The Royal Academy of Music already existed and was followed by the the Royal College of Organists in 1864, Trinity in 1872, the predecessor of the Royal College of Music in 1873, and Guildhall in 1880. Through their graded systems of local examinations it became possible for spare-time students to obtain high qualifications in performance and teaching: indeed the Associated Board offered this to the furthest-flung parts of empire. In the Isle of Man, as elsewhere, those who combined home music-teaching, the training of church choirs and playing the organ with other occupations, were able to acquire nationally recognised qualifications. Thus, when the Music Guild began, there were many such people to take a leading part in it.

The first "Music Guild" was held in the Palace Pavilion, a wooden hall on Douglas promenade between Castle Mona and the castellated entrance to Falcon Cliff. (Photos reproduced by kind permission of S R Keig Ltd)

The competitive music festival movement

It was in 1882 that the first competitive music festival was founded in Stratford, London, by John Curwen, the son of the founder of the Tonic Sol Fa industry. He was motivated by his experience as an adjudicator at the Welsh National Eisteddfod, which had been recently revived as an instrument of Welsh cultural and political aspirations. However, even though such eisteddfods were set up outside the Principality, the English music festival movement was independent of them, and was brought together in 1905 when the Association of Music Competition Festivals (later the the British Federation of Music Festivals) was founded through the work of Miss Mary Wakefield, a wealthy professional singer who started a festival in 1885 at her home village near Grange over Sands. It was an adjunct to a flower show, but bloomed into the Kendal Music Festival, which inspired Miss M L Wood to consult Miss Wakefield and found the music competitions in the Isle of Man Fine Arts and Industrial Guild. A plaque in memory of Mary Wakefield became one of the Manx festival's trophies.

Competition was seen as the natural means of improvement in all spheres of Victorian life, and Miss Wakefield's system set out to bring together competing choirs with the ultimate object of a combined performance which would raise the standards of local music. In the *Manx Sun* of 1892, she wished the new venture success, but warned that the only enemy of her scheme was jealousy, and as church competed against church, village against village and school against school, jealously did emerge, while a century later it is by no means unheard of.

While the Manx Music Festival is not the first such festival to reach its centenary, it may well be the first to have run for that time without a break. The Kendal festival came to be held in alternate years, and the Stratford festival closed for four years during the second world war. Likewise the Mrs Sunderland Festival, founded in 1889, could not take place in 1940 as large public gatherings were discouraged for fear of air raids.

The circumstances which led to the founding of festivals were varied: the last-named one arose from the golden-wedding celebrations of a Brighouse-born singer of national reputation. The Manx festival is unique in that it was tacked on to an annual exhibition of art and industry, whose own origins were part of another national movement

The Guild: a serious object of usefulness

Following the Great Exhibition at the Crystal Palace, concern for standards of industrial and domestic design led to the setting up of national and local museums and colleges where good principles of design and craftsmanship could be taught. Ripples in this great tide in the affairs of industrial man reached the shores of the Isle of Man and in 1876 the Douglas School of Art was founded.

In 1888 the Isle of Man Fine Arts and Industrial Guild came into being. The very name of Guild, the organisation of medieval craftsmen, links it to the doctrines of William Morris and John Ruskin, who called for a return to traditional craftsmanship as practised before factory methods of production, thus restoring the dignity and creativity of the artisan. This movement was a fashionable hobby for gentlefolk with pretensions to good taste and a bent for handicraft. In the Isle of Man such people must have been impressed by Ruskin, despite his socialism, for he had encouraged the local artists Nicholson and Swinnerton, and founded the Laxey Woollen Mills.

The minute book of the Fine Arts and Industrial Guild for 1892 states:

"The intention of the founders had been to foster in the working classes a love of art, to encourage industry in their own homes. The working classes however, had not been influenced to the extent hoped for, but rather stood aloof, at least as friendly onlookers rather than fellow workers, supposing that the ladies were

This title page for the festival programme, first used in 1927, was designed by Archibald Knox, an early exhibitor in the Fine Arts and Industrial Guild whose work is how held in international esteem.

doing so rather for their own amusement than some serious object of usefulness."

Among the gentlemen of the committee were prominent businessmen and politicians. There was Robert Swann Stephen, who was a lawyer and commander of the Rifle Volunteers; Phillip Christian, an architect and builder; John Mylrea, lawyer and accomplished musician; the architect Armitage Rigby; Dalrymple Maitland who was proprietor of two Liverpool newspapers, and Colonel Freeth who was the Chief Constable. Less typical was John Miller Nicholson, the Royal Academician who was a master painter and decorator.

The ladies included a formidable collection of carriage folk. There was Miss Goldie-Taubman, whose father was the leading landed proprietor. Other stately homes were represented by Miss Gawne of Kentraugh, Miss Crellin of Orrisdale, Miss Moore of Cronkbourne, and Mrs Drinkwater of Kirby who, like Mrs Gill, was the wife of a deemster (as the Manx judges are called).

Of Mrs Fleming it had to be said that while her husband was in trade, being a master butcher, they did live at a big house called *Harcroft* and that must have commanded a curtsey.

It is also possible that some of the lower orders they hoped to persuade to practise art and industry, preferred to be out drinking the product which bore the names of two other committee ladies: Mrs Okell and Mrs Clinch.

It is these Manx worthies that posterity should thank for accepting Miss Wood's proposal. Already there was serious musical activity, and it was the basis for a new "serious object of usefulness". All that was needed was a good organiser and soon they found this in the person of Mrs Florence Laughton.

The first ten years

Florence Laughton was the wife of the High Bailiff (stipendiary magistrate) of Peel. In 1891 when her husband lost his seat in the Keys (the Manx House of Commons) to a local hero, Joseph Mylcheest the Diamond King, she declared that she would no longer organise good works for the ungrateful electorate. Peel's loss was the Island's gain, for she became secretary of the Music section of the Guild in 1893 and was secretary or treasurer for well over 30 years.

The first Music Guild lasted one day and admission cost two old pence. There was a prize of one pound for the conductor of the winning choir and bronze medals for its members. Members of the winning children's choir received a white-metal medal, some of which are known still to exist. There were also classes for sight reading and composing a hymn tune.

Afterwards, a conference with the conductors was held. Miss Wood insisted that December clashed with the Christmas preparations of church choirs and wanted to move the music section, and if need be the entire Guild, to the spring. Headmaster Fielding was adamant that after Christmas the schools would not be able to devote time to the Guild. He may have been concerned about examinations and inspections which determined the school grant and the teachers' pay.

It was contended that the judge should be

placed in a booth so that he could not see the choirs and should not be told who he was listening to, and there were demands that he provide a report for publication "showing in what points the competitors had excelled and in what they had failed". It is an indication of the enthusiasm of those judges that they were prepared to travel from as far as London and brave the Irish Sea in December to do all this and conduct the concert, for a fee which, inclusive of travel expenses, was "not to exceed five guineas".

It was a condition of entry for senior choirs that they must all learn the concert piece and perform together. Some choristers objected to having to buy this music as well as their competition piece, so it was agreed to lend concert music free, or to provide it at a discount.

For the second concert it was agreed to pay two local soloists a guinea each, but if the only suitable tenor was not available, one from across the water would be sought for up to ten pounds. Six months later one of these local soloists had not returned money for concert tickets sold, with the result that Novello's bill of five pounds for concert music could not be paid.

It was decided that anyone could sing in two choirs provided they were genuine members, and that people who mainly earned their living through music should not sing, although they were permitted to conduct. Classes for string quartets and vocal quartets were introduced.

Despite the success of the music competitions, the concert had been a failure because of the noise in the hall while other people were still looking at the exhibits. Furthermore the stage was no longer large enough for all the choirs

taking part. It was decided to clear away the exhibition and set out chairs, and to ballot for a quota from each choir to perform.

The first vocal solo classes were held in 1894, and admission was raised to six old pence (2$\frac{1}{2}$p) and twice that for a reserved seat. Another measure of the Music Guild's growing popularity was that the committee felt able to turn down a request from the clergy to shift the date by a week to avoid clashing with a big Mission.

In 1895 Miss Wood got her way and the senior music section moved to the spring. It seems that the choirs had insufficient time to get into shape between the end of the visiting season and mid-December. By this time too some of them were likely also to be involved in the Christmas productions of the new Choral Union, which was founded to perform oratorio but soon turned to operetta. For the time being the children's music section remained in December, and by 1896 some country schools were closing to take part in it.

From the start there had been a good train service to Port Erin and Peel and to Ramsey via Kirk Michael, but in 1894 the electric railway reached Laxey, then a thriving mining centre, and its population was able to participate more fully.

By 1987 there were 12 senior classes, requiring a second day and justifying the forming of a full music committee which appears to have been separate in all but name from the parent Guild. Two years later there were events for specifically Manx songs, and elocution classes soon followed. They were judged by High Bailiff Laughton, whom history records as being very fond of the sound of his own voice.

In l902 the new Palace Ballroom opened. A soloist's gold medal won that year by Tom Longton has survived. Having come to the Island and married a Manx girl, he was a chorister, organist, a clarinettist in the Rifle Volunteer Band, and played leading roles in the Choral Union productions. His son became a chorister, as did his daughter Isobel Callow, whose husband was a church organist for 50 years. Their two daughters competed when young as vocalists, pianists, violinists, and in elocution and drama. One is still in choirs. There have been many such families.

The mother of Manx music

When she arrived from London in 1857, aged 16, Miss M L Wood was already well-educated

The Palace Ballroom, opened in l902, made it possible to have up to 4,000 people at the Music Guild concerts. (Photo reproduced by kind permission of S R Keig Ltd)

Miss M L Wood presiding over a choir. It is said that she recommended gargling with stewed apples to loosen the vocal chords. (Photo reproduced by kind permission of Manx National Heritage)

musically. Ten years later she became a Tonic Sol Fa enthusiast, and gathered together classes of 200 in Douglas, 100 in Peel and even got to work on the garrison soldiers in Castletown. She was barely 30 when a newspaper prophetically declared "Miss Woods is an institution: the historian of the Island chronicling the manners and customs of the Victorian era must make honourable mention of her".

Long before she founded the Music Guild, she ran a choir which gave charity concerts, but she seems to have disbanded it because of lack of response to her efforts. However her Diocesan Choral festival in Peel Castle, the site of the ruined cathedral, was considered a great success. She became organist and choir mistress at Kirk Braddan and published a ballad in that church's honour, as well as making choral arrangements of the Manx national anthem and its rival song *Ellan Vannin*. She played the organ for the

Tynwald Day state service, and when the best-selling novelist Hall Caine, who was then in the Keys, complained about the state of St John's chapel organ, she tartly pointed out in her music column in the *Manx Sun* that he could easily afford to give the £200 needed for a new one. Once she conducted the Choral Union's *Mikado* but dourly declared that light opera was neither improving nor elevating.

She taught music at the Douglas High School and its Pupil Teacher Centre, thus ensuring a high standard of future music teaching in schools, and in 1910 she was presented with a testimonial purse of £200, which would have been enough to live on in comfort for a year. After her death a memorial fund was set up to assist promising Guild competitors. It still pays the original sum of five pounds, which would have paid for at least a term's music lessons when it began. A plaque in Douglas library commemorates Miss Wood as *The Mother of Manx Music*.

She was sternly critical of the musical standards she had manifestly raised: " ... although the Music Guild has done much to improve music, still there is too much of the competing spirit and too little of the real love of singing ... sight singing has always been a weak subject amongst Manx singers."

Early orchestras

Throughout the festival's existence there have always been pianists who are the official accompanists to the singers, but since their contribution is by its nature self-effacing, it seldom features in newspaper reports. This is in contrast to the orchestras which accompanied the choral concerts, and which in the early days were organised by Harry Wood. His namesake, the Mother of Manx Music, was not impressed by them, stating: "Instrumental music generally is at a low ebb. It is deplorable that we have not a band capable of accompanying such difficult music as is now set for the Guild concert."

When he was 16 Harry Wood, who had already been in the Leeds Grand Theatre orchestra, became solo violinist at a Douglas music hall and in 1902 became musical director for the Palace and Derby Castle Company. There he enjoyed more than local fame through his compositions of popular songs and dances and his association with music hall singer Florrie Forde.

In winter he was the orchestral mainstay of amateur entertainments, and he founded an independent brass band competition. In 1931 he conducted in the first broadcast concert from the Island, during which a recording was made of *Manx Rhapsody*, composed by his brother Haydn, and this was frequently heard on the radio.

Haydn Wood, best known as the composer of *Roses of Picardy*, had been one of Harry Wood's violin pupils, and another brother, Thomas, became flute professor at the Royal College of Music. They both played in Harry Wood's bands.

In 1904 the Music Guild lobby persuaded the Baume Trustees, who were administering a fortune left to charity by a miserly Frenchman residing in Douglas, to award a scholarship for three or four years at the Royal Academy of Music. At the time its £50 per annum was quite adequate. The first to benefit was a pupil of

Many of the members of this orchestra, founded by Frank Heslop (end of front row) played in the Music Guild concerts. Harry Wood is first on back row. James Burman (Government Secretary) is fourth from left on front row. Fred Poulter (third from left back row) and T P Fargher (third from right middle row) used to play in the Guild concert while the choirs they had trained sang under the adjudicator's baton. (Photo, taken about 1892, reproduced by kind permission of Manx National Heritage)

Harry Wood. His name was Samuel Robinson, and he became a broadcasting violinist under the Manx professional name of Orry Corjeag. His headmaster was Richard Lace, who was to be a church organist for 66 years, and he wrote in the Kirk Michael school log book: "Samuel Robinson, who took two firsts and one second prize at the Guild, was highly praised by Lady Raglan. Her Ladyship paid him a visit in his cottage home and along with Mrs Stratton (the bishop's wife) is about to cause him to undergo a thorough musical education."

Harry Wood depended on local amateurs and his own pupils for the Guild concerts, for unlike festivals elsewhere he could not draw on nearby professionals in concert orchestras and theatre bands. Despite this the 1910 adjudicator paid a curious compliment: "They played most admirably and were quite adequate for the task ... the difficulty of importing outside help is one of the strongest assets the festival possesses."

Harry Wood's successors as orchestra leader were his own pupil Kathleen Ryding, who also became a violin teacher: and J E Quayle, who made lifelong endeavours to keep alive amateur orchestras and music appreciation. "Quayle Mus Bac", as he was known, made settings of Manx folk tunes and two of his longer classical works were performed at Guild concerts in the 1940s.

The centre of all musical work

It was the same adjudicator who declared that the secretary was a genius and everything went like clockwork. Judging by the comments of G F Clucas, a Speaker of the Keys who was chairman of the Guild committee for many years, Florence Laughton achieved this with a firmness and hauteur befitting a High Bailiff's lady. In 1907 she was invited to give a paper at the third annual conference of the Association of Music Competition Festivals, and gave a comprehensive account of the financial and educational success of the Music Guild.

She reported that one of the objects was to interest all classes and to educate the audience as well as the competitors, so if a higher price for admission were charged, much popular interest would be lost.

Total receipts were around £400, of which £190 was for the concert, to which admission cost from one shilling to two shillings. Entry fees from up to 300 competitors raised £15. An annual appeal raised some £50 for prizes, which ranged from £10 for the chief choral award to £1 for soloists. There was usually up to £50 in hand when all expenses were paid, and these included extra travelling expenses of judges, and half the travel expenses for out-of-town choirs.

Out of surplus funds, grants were made towards student's studies (a sum revealed in 1910 to total £365 over 10 years), while help was given to choirs competing in English festivals. The secretary concluded by saying: "We have become the centre of all musical work and interest in the Island ... We have a colony of students (in London) and our young people feel that the Insular competitions are but a first stepping stone in their musical careers and our competitions flourish accordingly."

About that time there was a Manx student string quartet in London. There were 124 insular candidates for the various grades of Trinity College and a Peel school had 14 violinists.

By 1912, the year when the "Coming of Age" was celebrated in style, there were 26 competition classes in the Guild. The previous few years had been marked by the successes of Guild-bred choirs at English festivals, but despite this there was some criticism. *The Isle of Man Times* pontificated: "Care must be taken lest legitimate pride degenerates into silly self-satisfaction ... a fine voice is a wasted gift unless there is a readiness to cultivate it by some degree of musical education, to sink a certain amount of individuality, and work in concert with others in order to render good music worthily."

The "Coming of Age" was celebrated by presenting winners with a souvenir bronze plaque, showing The Viking's Homecoming surrounded by other Manx national symbols.

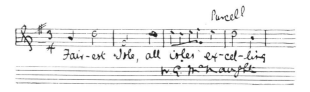

A special message was composed and drawn by Lady Raglan for the programme, and past adjudicators sent musical greetings. This one was from Doctor McNaught, senior HM Inspector of Schools Music.

Another commentator wrote: "Musical existence is manifested but once a year, apparent death and disintegration supervening until the time for preparation for the next competition." He pleaded for competition to become the means of forming a permanent choir of 150 which "by using the entire musical wisdom of the Island, could present major choral works throughout the year, using which ever of the leading conductors was best for the particular work".

The politics of music

In the early years of this century, the Music Guild was also a focus for national pride. This pride had two aspects: the ability to compete creditably in mainland festivals against the very towns which invaded the Island in holiday wakes weeks, and patriotism as expressed in Manx national music. Such patriotism was usually expressed within the greater loyalty for Crown and Empire, for few families were without relatives in the dominions and colonies.

However, for some there was growing distaste for the political system which was eulogised in the Manx national anthem as "Thy throne of Home Rule", and personified in Governor Raglan, who, like Pooh Bah in the *Mikado*, controlled all aspects of government. Others could not reconcile the economic benefits of the visiting industry with its effect on the traditional Manx way of life, be it in the loosening of morals or the loss of the Manx language.

Those who participated in the early Music Guild were among the first to have literature about their Island, and this included the poems of T E Brown, which even an Oxford professor thought had their place in the annals of English literature.

In 1896 W H Gill published his *Manx National Song Book*. It included some traditional folk tunes transformed with musical modes acceptable to the pianoforte's scales and polite lyrics. Such national songs were advocated by the English Board of Education, which inspected Manx schools by invitation. Its inspector was A P Graves, who had Manx family connections and had written some of the lyrics in the *Manx National Song Book*.

Bringing home the shields

Joseph Looney was a self-taught musician who, although a tailor by trade, was a church organist and taught music at Douglas Grammar School. According to his obituary in 1919 he was "the greatest force, so far as music is concerned ever produced in the Isle of Man... he achieved brilliance as a trainer of choristers".

In 1902 he took a choir of 150 to the Welsh Eisteddfod and came back with the tidings that the Manx, although placed fourth, had been judged worthy of musical recognition alongside the great choirs of Wales. He began to take choirs to the Morecambe Festival at a time when Edward Elgar was adjudicating there, so that Manx choristers shared some of the credit for the great man's proclamation that "the centre of music is not London but somewhere further north".

In the spring of 1907, Mr Looney's all-Island choir won the major award at Morecambe, and then in the autumn it won the Challenge Shield at Blackpool. The choir and its supporters set off like an expeditionary force in chartered steamers and its victorious return in the small hours was greeted by the crowd that had gathered at the pier, to the strains of *Bringing Home The Shield.*

While one Island critic wrote that "The adjudicators laid themselves open to a charge of extravagance for granting the maximum marks for the first three pieces", others agreed with the judgment of the man who had shouted out in the Blackpool concert-hall "The Isle of Man's first: the rest is nowhere!"

At the Liverpool Manx Association gala concert which quickly followed, there were speeches which not only boasted of Manx musical superiority over the English but also over the Welsh, who were at the concert in force.

Later there was a similar concert in Douglas,

and every chorister was presented with a commemorative gold medal. Joseph Looney declined some of his own testimonial purse to make this possible, as public response to the appeal was not generous. However, after his death a memorial medallion, designed by Knox, was instituted for conductors who had competed in the Manx Music Festival for three successive years.

There was more patriotic exultation in 1909 when Noah Moore's Douglas Male Voice Choir won a major award at Blackpool, resulting in the offer of an American tour which it was unable to accept because of the problems of absence from work.

The Music Guild was enjoying social and patriotic cachet though the enthusiastic support of the Governor and Lady Raglan, who usually occupied their throne-like seats of honour throughout the festival. She wrote programme

Joseph Looney's choir on the occasion of the Liverpool concert. Mr Looney is seated on St George's Hall steps between the Morecambe and Blackpool Challenge Shields. The girl on the left, in a place of honour as the youngest chorister, is Ethel Caine, the author's mother.

The Queen and the Choirs.

ROYAL CONGRATULATION FOR MANX SINGERS.

The Honourable Charlotte Knollys, the Queen's private secretary, has written as follows to Mrs. Laughton, honorary secretary of the Manx Musical Festival :—

I have had the pleasure of submitting your letter and the syllabus of your next festival to her Majesty the Queen, and I am commanded by her Majesty to assure you of the great interest taken by the Queen in the Manx choirs. Her Majesty is also much pleased to hear of the signal success which has attended their performances this year, and congratulates them specially on having brought home both the Morecambe and Blackpool shields.

October 29th, 1907.

A. R. GAUL.

God sent His sing - - - - ers up - - on earth.

News of the Blackpool victory was sent to Queen Alexandra in the hope of a Royal Command performance, but the reply, reproduced in the following year's programme, dashed such hopes.

notes comparing the beauties of the Island's music with its scenery and extolling the uplifting qualities of both, and when handing out the prizes, he joked about village rivalries and his bucolic musical tastes. He even rebuked the Agricultural Society for "preferring to hear a bull's bellow than the sweet strains of music" when it had arranged a show which clashed with the Guild. This was quite remarkable from a gentleman whose eye for a pedigree beast was well known.

It was in 1908 that Manchester Manx Society gave the first challenge shield, and by 1914 the Liverpool, Vancouver and Transvaal societies had done likewise. All these were for choirs: the coveted medal for soloists (shown on the back cover of this book) was not to come from Cleveland, Ohio until after the Great War. In 1911 Florence Laughton became founding secretary of the new World Manx Association, and in the following year the Manchester Manx presented her with its silver medal for service to the Manx people. Her successor as Music Guild secretary, Willy Craine, attributed this flow of trophies to the fact that "there are many former competitors who are now exiles, who never forget the ex-

A Guild choir, name and date unknown, outside Villa Marina House with Joseph Looney. He had started making music as a very small boy by banging on three horse-shoes in a Foxdale farmyard. (Photo reproduced by kind permission of Manx National Heritage)

In 1908 Crosby village was the first winner of the Manchester Shield and retained it the next year. Its conductor was W A Craine and he walked back to Onchan for some 50 rehearsals to achieve this. He was secretary of the Manx Music Festival for about 45 years. (Photo reproduced by kind permission of Manx National Heritage)

traordinary enthusiasm which prevails in Music Festival week". An illustration of this was a published letter from an exile telling how, on Guild Night, he had dreamed that he was on the Palace stage again, receiving his award.

No language — no nation

The Manx Language Society (now the Manx Society) was founded in 1899. Preservation of folk music was high among its objectives, and that year at the Guild there were classes for Manx songs and bible readings, and a Manx concert with that Pan-Celtic celebrity, the Abbé Fournier, giving the prizes.

Before long there were reputable Guild pieces which introduced Manx culture to the musical mainstream. They included Elgar's setting of T E Brown's *Weary Wind of the West*, the same poet's *When Childer Plays* to music by Walford Davies, and Arthur Somerville's setting of *Mylecharane*. Harry and Haydn Wood, Miss M L Wood, Walter Gill and lesser mortals also contributed, and a contemporary list shows 54 such effusions. They ranged from *I'm The Pride of Port le Murra* and *God Bless Our Anniversary Day* to numerous laments for *Illiam Dhone* and the *Sheep Under The Snow*.

The programme for the Manx Music Festival,

The Vancouver Shield for children's choirs.

officially so-named around 1909, appeared with its name also in the Manx language, and led by Peel's Sophia Morrison, the Manx Language Society published music for a Guild class called "Traditional music hitherto unpublished" and contributed to the expense of this class. However in 1912 this category was cancelled by the festival committee, but the existing classes for established songs in Manx attracted a remarkable 240 entries that year.

Then in 1914 Sir Edward Elgar OM was the adjudicator. Lady Elgar confided to her diary that her husband "adjudicated very well and said nice things to people", but the truth is that he made some crushing remarks.

When a boys' choir sang Bantock's *Road to Fairyland*, they must have been puzzled when he complained: "I came here hoping to see fairies, and I hoped to find young people who had been singing about fairyland in childlike sympathy with the elfin world. I fear these children do not dream the dreams of my youth."

After hearing a solo test-piece, he enquired, "Where are the Romeos of the Isle of Man? Evidently not among its tenors." However not all performers displeased him, and he awarded full marks to Noah Moore in the baritone solo.

For the final concert, Elgar conducted his own

work, *The Banner of St George*, in respect of which Lady Elgar wrote, presumably with irony, that the orchestra was extraordinary. Then Sir Edward opened his speech by commending proposals to form a Manx National choir and declared "You have the material for it to take its place among the great choirs of the world". Needless to say this was greeted with tumultuous applause.

What he then said about Manx folk music must be considered in the light of his own views on such music generally. He never used folk themes in his classical works, and a few weeks earlier an influential critic had proclaimed that "the spirit that would overtake the achievements of Elgar" was to be found in the utilisation of folk music by Vaughan Williams, who did so in accordance with Arts and Crafts principles. Furthermore, one of the test pieces Elgar had to judge was a Manx folk tune harmonised by Vaughan Williams, who had been a recent adjudicator.

This is what Elgar said: "You possess, and you have given us, specimens of Manx music ... It does not amount to very much ... these simple melodies appeal to your hearts as they could not do to a foreigner ... This old music, touching as it is, finds its real expression in its homes ... it is not always suited to the concert room. As specimens of composition they bear the same relationship to modern music as astrology does to astronomy — interesting but too antiquated to be of practical use."

Such strictures from a man of his standing must have been a blow to those who were devoted to Manx folk music and the language it

was sung in, but a few months later it was no patriotic melody by Elgar that became the marching song of the British army in France, but a ditty which legend says was first used by soldiers on summer camp in the Isle of Man who sang it as they marched to the boat upon mobilisation.

kione jiarg

Apyrn doo, Apyrn doo,
Vel oo cheet ? Vel oo cheet ?
Skee fieau, skee fieau,
Lhondoo, Lhondoo.

Red head, red head,
Black apron, black apron,
Are you coming ? Are you coming ?
Tired waiting, tired waiting,
Blackbird, Blackbird.

Manx folk songs, such as this one illustrated by Archibald Knox in Sophie Morrison's Manx Fairy Tales, did not please Sir Edward Elgar in 1914.

They had heard *Tipperary* from Florrie Forde and Harry Wood's band.

At the first war-time festival, Governor Raglan prevailed on all able-bodied young male choristers to answer the call of king and country, and the others to devote their spare time to guarding the enemy internees, pointing out that what mattered was not that the Music Guild survived, but that the country did. In the event the festival did take place throughout the war, and the Raglans supported it as a relaxation from privation and sorrow and an occasion of patriotic unity.

It is hard to understand therefore, why in 1916 the festival committee, while introducing a new competition for a patriotic song, swept away the classes for Manx language folk songs, which for many were their expression of patriotism. According to the Manx Language Society, there was no explanation or discussion. Whatever the reason, it must have been a blow for those whose motto was "No Language — No Nation".

A united heart and voice

In the later years of the war, Lady Raglan gave thanks in her programme notes that "as a Guild we are able to count on a united heart and voice to promote the sweet harmony of our beloved little Manx nation". The Governor's prize-giving speeches called for music that was "more cheerful and more martial to show that we are not downhearted" and declared that "wherever there are Manxmen shouldering a rifle, their thoughts will be with us tonight".

Assurances were issued that all male performers were either medically unfit or exempt from call-up as key workers in the war effort. It may have been the shortage of such contestants that led to the introduction of Morris dancing, nursery rhymes and action songs, but there was also a new class for War Workers Ladies Choirs. The Palace was occupied by such a factory, and the last wartime festival attracted the biggest audience ever to the new Villa Marina concert hall.

In l915 Onchan won the Lowey Cup, the Wakefield Medallion, the Manchester Shield and the Transvaal Shield. One of the two gentlemen in the centre may be conductor Lieutenant Cullerne. (Photo courtesy of Onchan Village Commissioners, per Peter Kelly.)

Chapter 2

1919-1928:
From victory to the Depression

Shortly after the end of the war, the Governor, together with Lady Raglan, departed in the wake of the constitutional reforms he had strenuously opposed. Yet even those who had recently demonstrated against him at the Tynwald ceremony and in a general strike, must have regretted the loss of such enthusiastic patrons of the music festival.

The first peace-time festival took £473 admission money, leaving some £150 in hand. It was reported that while "even yet some of the most tuneful voices are engaged in foreign parts, others have demonstrated that the stern work in which they have been taking part has not blunted their devotion to the science of sweet sounds."

The prize-giving night became a national victory celebration when Manchester Manx Society medals were awarded for services to the Manx people. One went to Leigh Goldie-Taubman for his welfare work for servicemen's families, while another went to the Rev Copeland-Smith for organising the war-effort clothing production which had alleviated female unemployment. The greatest applause however was heard when Miss M L Wood came up for her medal. Her Music Guild had kept the home fires burning.

In 1920, when there was a summer harvest of well over half a million visitors, it seemed that everything was getting back to normal. Even when the Palace Ballroom burnt down, everyone was confident that the heroes of the building trade would have a new one built for the next season. But quite apart from the missing male singers, the Guild would never be like it used to be. Lady Fry, wife of the new Governor, was more interested in the Girl Guide movement than music; Mrs Laughton, though still treasurer, no longer lived on the Island, while Joseph Looney was doubtless conducting the great big Manx choir in the sky.

Notes of discord

As the 1921 festival was about to take place, industrial unrest resulted in a coal strike which disrupted trains and shipping. Some may have been sorry that Mr Field Hyde did manage to get through to adjudicate. He declared that he did not know how many of the sopranos were in love, but they needed to be if they were to sing the test piece well: an insensitive remark in view of the loss of so many men in the war. He also informed one young lady that while she did have a nice voice, she was too proud of it. If she was, it may have been justifiable, for she became the first woman to win the Cleveland medal three times.

The schoolteachers had laboured long and hard to launch the first-ever Children's festival and concert, but faced with only one entry in the nursery rhyme class, this adjudicator fatuously asked if children were playing golf or motorcycling nowadays. This was at the time when such juveniles as Dan Minay and Doris Lowthian were appearing in the Guild and a teenager named Douglas Buxton was making his debut in the tenor solo. All were to add lustre to the festival in years to come.

The second Children's festival involved such numbers that the Sunday School staging of Victoria Street and Rose Mount chapels had to be hired. Some thought that this event was not

A choir conducted by Noah Moore in the Palace Ballroom in 1915.

The Children's festival concert around 1927. This photo, together with that on page 33, reproduced by kind permission of the Manx Heritage Foundation, provides a comparison between the 1902 Palace and its successor, which was renamed the Lido.

worth such expense and would only take custom from the choral concert. Nor were the new classes for small orchestras and brass ensembles attracting much interest.

The Isle of Man Examiner offered a guinea for the best letter on how to improve the festival. The winner was Arthur Dick who asserted that the Guild had made no progress at all in his 30 years as a chorister and soloist because the test-pieces chosen by the adjudicators were so unsuitable. He called for a Competitors' Union to choose the music and claimed that the Guild would soon be a thing of the past unless the undemocratic committee ceased making secret decisions and started listening to the advice of younger folk. He suggested that male-voice choir competitions should be run at times which would not interfere with earning a living, and that since professional soloists could be heard in plenty in the summer they should be dispensed with in the festival concert and the fees used to give bigger cash prizes.

At the ensuing AGM the secretary pointed out that there was more democracy than had been suggested, since every donor could take part in electing the committee and every competing choir could send a spokesman. He also revealed that the Cleveland Manx Society, which had lately enhanced the prizes for the Special solo classes, was considering a further gift of an undecided nature.

The Cleveland Test

On the eve of the 1923 festival there was surprise that for the first time in 13 years Onchan Village was not entering a choir, and that Noah Moore was not entering a single one either. The prospect of the Cleveland gold medal to be competed for by the six winners of the Special solo classes did not capture the imagination of the press.

The adjudicator was the popular singer Peter Dawson, and he declared that Allan Quirk, the first winner of the Cleveland medal, was capable of becoming a great singer. Behind a winning performer there is usually a talented teacher, and in this case it was Miss Effie Fayle, who will be remembered by those who sang in her various children's choirs. For the second Cleveland contest, scheduled to start at 9pm, enough interest was anticipated to hold back the trains until it was over. All the same, there were those who thought that it would only take money away from the big choral concert, as country folk would only come into Douglas for one evening.

A feeling arose that Cleveland medal winners should not enter for it again, which would have led to the Island's best singers being progressively eliminated from the public eye. After a few years the committee decided to encourage past winners to enter again, as this would have the box-office appeal that was urgently needed.

Consequently there was great excitement in 1932 when Allan Quirk and Margaret Minay, each of whom had won twice, qualified for the contest, and Allan fulfilled Peter Dawson's prophesy by becoming the first triple-winner. There was more excitement the following year when the adjudicators could not make up their mind between Margaret Minay (by then Mrs Bull) and Mona Clucas, who was just 21. They took the unprecedented step of asking both to sing again and the young lady from Peel won.

A year later Margaret Bull did win for the third time. She qualified to compete by her sixth Special solo win. This beat the record of five held by her father Fred Minay who, since he also had singing sons, was described in the press as "head of the Island's greatest singing family". By this time the Cleveland Manx Society was concerned that its medal might not be worn with such pride by those who had won it more than once, and suggested that it should be withheld in such circumstances and a lesser prize given. In contrast some aficionados were all for a special extra prize for triple-winners, and a super contest open to Cleveland medalists only.

Fortuitously, some 30 years passed before more triple winners emerged, and there are now in this category Mrs E Gelling, Mrs Eleanor Shimmin, Peter Cringle and Graham Crowe. In 1968 Allan Wilcocks became the first to win it four times, and the press pointed out that his father had named him after the first man to win it three times.

Victory In London

When Noah Moore's Douglas Ladies Choir won the London Dawnay Shield in 1924, he had left schoolteaching to become manager of the municipally-owned Villa Marina, to which he was to bring some of the world's leading singers for its summer Sunday night concerts. In the early days of his rise to fame, the Guild sometimes seemed to be a contest between him and his brother, a Peel headmaster, to see which of them would win the most choral classes.

On the occasion of this first Dawnay Shield win, the Mayor of Douglas, who had accompanied the choir, delivered himself of a victory speech to the London Manx Society. The choir no sooner got home than it was invited back to broadcast in the presence of Queen Mary, who duly expressed her appreciation of her musical Manx subjects.

Douglas Corporation and the Island's tourist publicity department then decided to contribute £150 each towards the choir's additional travelling expenses. Presumably they hoped that, in return for their outlay, some of the three million listeners would be inspired to take their holidays in the Isle of Man. However it was reported that the lack of local public enthusiasm when the choir returned was a disgrace to the town. Nor was the subsequent Guild concert, which featured its Dawnay test-pieces, well attended. Could it have been that Noah Moore was getting the "Manx crabs" treatment and being pulled down in case he got to the top? After all, the forthcoming dedication of Douglas war memorial was due to give him pride of place before Lord Derby and the highest of Manx society, for he was to conduct an assembly of 3,000 schoolchildren.

Noah Moore and Douglas Ladies did bring home the Dawnay Shield three times in all, and before long Mrs Mary Purcell Black's Ramsey Cushag Choir had done the same. Ramsey gave them a royal welcome, even to a brass band playing *See the Conquering Heroes Come.*

Future in melting pot

In 1926, with nearly 2,800 competitors spread

Douglas Ladies Choir on the occasion of its London broadcast. Noah Moore is in centre of front row, and the Dawnay Shield is top right. (Photo reproduced by kind permission of Manx National Heritage)

over four days and with 250 donors, the future of the festival seemed assured. There was a piano competition between the winners of the past four years, the prize being a piano presented by Blakemore's Music Shop. A new brass band class, in which both a quickstep and a hymn had to be performed, attracted mainland contestants and was reported to be an occasion of great enthusiasm.

However, that summer the General Strike took place and visitors were down in number by over 150,000. This must have hit the future spending power of many of those Guild week enthusiasts whom one paper had described so romantically: "Whenever one saw in the hand of any man, woman or child braving the Douglas streets a folded booklet in vivid red, one knew very well where the bearer was bound, and one saw this so perpetually that the red almost danced before one's eyes at bedtime." Apparently one didn't notice the travelling rugs and hot water bottles some of them were also carrying, and it was left to a letter to the editor a few years later to point out that the best way to combat falling attendances was to heat the concert hall.

In 1927 adjudicator John Ireland warned of the danger of gramophones and wireless sets in practically every house, fearing that they might "become a substitute for acquiring musical facility". Many things seemed to be getting blamed for enticing the public away from the festival, but presumably not football, for that was the year when Castletown Wanderers won the Manx football cup final, fielded a choir in the Guild and later played away to score at the Blackpool Music Festival.

In the 1928 Childrens' festival there was a mass performance of a new work called *O Vannin, Ellan Vannin* by a Ramsey headmaster. It was reported laconically that his libretto was well suited to his setting of a carval (Manx folk hymn) of sombre mode. Neither that evening nor the main concert with its guest appearance of the victorious Ramsey Cushags choir was a box-office success. There was a marked decline in choral entries, which some attributed to pot-hunting at the London festival shortly before the Manx one. One paper made the acid comment that, while there were soloists in plenty, "half of them were indifferent and many would make no future contribution to the musical life of the Island. Notwithstanding their natural aptitude for singing, the Manx will not sacrifice other pleasures, the lure of the whist drive and the dance".

At the subsequent AGM it was even asserted that the new country bus services were luring country folk away from the Guild rather than to it, and a press report asked if the future of the Guild was in the melting pot.

The year of the one pound profit

Over the previous four years, takings had declined from around £740 to £450, and the net profit had dropped from £131 to little more than a pound. Yet only a handful turned up for that AGM and to make matters worse T C Corris, a leading conductor and a head teacher, announced that the teachers' association intended to boycott the Guild. The recent adjudicator had condemned all school music teaching on the strength of his dissatisfaction with one competition, and Governor Hill in his prize-giving speech had said that the whole population should be concerned at the suspension of progress in school choirs if they hoped for future victories at other festivals. Then to add injury to insult, His Excellency proposed that specialist music teachers should be brought over to put things right.

Mr Corris rightly pointed out that most of the adult choirs were also conducted by schoolteachers, and after a motion was carried to have four teacher-representatives on the the committee, the boycott was withdrawn.

In the wake of this crisis, the newly-founded

Miss Effie Fayle (second from left on back row) was one of the many schoolteachers who entered children's and senior choirs.

Isle of Man Music Society declared that the "suspension in the progress of music which had been so noticeable at the Guild is only curable by such an institution as this Music Society, the object of which is to build up a body of musical opinion". Prominent in this society was Bertram Sargeaunt, the Government Secretary, and when presiding over the local Associated Board presentations, he again referred to the decline in musical accomplishment in young people. Warning that music, like religion, was in decline, he said he trembled to think what would happen to it in 20 or 30 years time. If he could have foreseen the futures of some of the young people who were receiving certificates that day, notably Emily Christian, he might have trembled with anticipation.

An anonymous letter to the editor blamed the ills of the Guild on the adjudicators' choices of test-pieces which were "melancholy, weird and lengthy items from weighty works". He accused them of all being cranks and faddists, with the exception of the one who had just "shown how fair-minded he was by confirming the opinion of the Cleveland audience, which has shown its keen appreciation and fine perception in acclaiming the victor". A leading article demanded that the second song in the Cleveland contest should also be a pre-ordained test piece since "anyone could stroll and perform some hackneyed song that has not entailed a moment of special study, and walk off with the the the medal".

Chapter 3

1929-1960:
The singing, dancing, acting years

By the end of the 1920s, in the Isle of Man as elsewhere, there were flourishing dancing schools which taught young ladies everything from ballet to tap dancing and the latest jazz craze, thereby offering them a strenuous but more sociable alternative to practising their scales.

For some years too, the *Isle of Man Examiner* had been running, in the full blaze of its own publicity, a very successful Ballroom Dancing Championship. Since it was on the very eve of the Manx Music Festival, it too may have been luring away some accomplished young people and their admirers.

In was in 1929 that the Guild committee had the acumen to accept that some forms of dance had a place among the muses and before long the winners of the adult classical dance were per-forming in the concert. In 1930 the talkies came to the Island, and thereafter, with all those great dance-musicals, the new competitions flourished. There were plaques and medals for budding Shirley Temples to compete for, and in the year of the Guild centenary, such mementos may raise incredulity in their recipients' grandchildren and regrets that this aspect of the festival has not survived into the Lloyd-Webber era.

The inclusion of dance in 1929 did not put the festival back on its feet, but at 2,900 the number of entries was slightly up, and Dr Moody, who was fulsome in his praise of the Children's festival, the country ladies choirs and the six Cleveland stars, appealed to everyone to keep the Guild going.

The early Thirties were the time of the Great Depression and of decline in the number of visitors to the Island, to which both government and business responded by investing in the tourist industry. Extensive improvements to harbours and promenades were started, airports were created, and new cinemas and steam-ships were built.

It may have been the hope that success there would give good publicity to tourism that led to renewed interest in competing at the Blackpool festival. These efforts were reported with such metaphors as "a formidable force under the Manx flag in the musical field, consisting of old campaigners who have successfully invaded in former years". There were also unsuccessful attempts to attract mainland groups to compete at the Manx festival with offers of special excursions and cheap travel. Appeals to Manx Societies to compete for their own challenge shields and challenges to other Dawnay Shield competitors to try to carry off the Manx

Opposite: Mrs A M Rushorth's 1934 dance entry. From left to right are Myrtle Copeland, Jean Canipa, Dena Wilson and Beryl Hardy. (Photo by courtesy of Mrs C E Conway, nee D Wilson)
Right: Sylvia Bailey and Mollie Skelly dancing in the 1930s. (Photo by courtesy of Mrs D Stott)

trophies also fell on deaf ears.

Six years after *Yn Chruinnaught* (The Gathering) had been brought into being by the World Manx Association and the Manx Language Society to provide opportunities for the performance of Manx culture, there arose a small but important place for it in the Guild. Its country dance competitions did give a potential platform for the Manx dances which were being collected by Mona Douglas. Then the English Folk Dance Society, led by the celebrated Arnold Foster, came over and ran a holiday course for would-be teachers. A few of them, notably Leighton Stowell who had long been an exponent of Morris dancing, introduced Manx dancing into their schools.

It was at the1930 Guild that the audience demanded an encore of the *Sword Dance of the Kings of Mann* by Billie Cain of Ramsey. He was Leighton's pupil and was asked to demonstrate it in London.

Dramatic change

In the early 1930's several new amateur dramatic societies came into being. They included the Legion Player, formed to produce *Journey's End*, and the Student Players, whose role in preparing law students for the drama of the courtroom was later commended by the press on the first court appearance of the future Deemster Luft.

The new Manx Amateur Dramatic Federation approached the Manx Music Festival Committee and in l933 the Guild launched a one-act play competition in the Coliseum, a theatre on the Palace site. With best seats at a shilling and free

admission to the pit, the six entries played to packed houses. The innovation was hailed by the press as "a triumph surpassing all expectation ... just what the organisers of this great national festival have been in search of for years to revive interest and enthusiasm".

It was also a boost for Manx culture, as the winning play was called *Mr Quilliam* by C Lee. While there was no shortage of such dialect plays on the village hall circuit, they were more notable for holding up a mirror to Manx nature than for dramatic potential. In this case the adjudicator said it was an astonishingly clever play and it also won a British Drama League competition and an international award in the USA.

The name of the festival was extended to include the word Drama, and Mr A H Teare presented a drama trophy. Soon there was another for dialect plays, and this became a stimulus for local playwrights. There was also a short-lived attempt to combine music and drama in a class for opera, in which the test-piece scene was performed in costume, with scenery and props provided.

There was some irritation when the celebrated but ancient thespian, Sir John Martin-Harvey, got so engrossed in hamming up excerpts from Victorian melodramas to show the local amateurs how to be proper actors, that it seemed he might never deliver his adjudications.

About this time, one paper conceded that live music was being studied by some children, "notwithstanding the march of the wireless", when an eight-year-old boy won both the under-12 violin and the under-14 piano classes. It so happened that this paper carried rhapsodic advertisements for the latest gramophone, the very device that later inspired this Master Fred Callow to become a jazz trumpeter.

Royal occasions

For the l935 Guild, veteran choristers dusted off their old scores of Elgar's *Banner of St George*, and a thousand sang it, aided by the Merseyside Sextet from the Liverpool Philharmonic Orchestra. The children had no such opportunity to celebrate the Silver Jubilee of King George and Queen Mary, for the schoolteachers had boycotted their festival concert as a protest against Tynwald's refusal to reinstate a previous pay cut. A subsequent adjudicator appealed to both parties to resolve the dispute for the sake of the musical future.

While the male followers of the festival were probably more interested in the fact that the Island's golfing champion, Mr J S Corrin, holed-in-one in the Cleveland contest, there must have been considerable speculation among the ladies as to what certain stars of the Guild were going to wear very soon at their weddings. In Jubilee week Mona Douglas married her music teacher, Duggie Buxton, and prize-winning dancer Sylvia Bailey married special tenor Donald Ashton. On the actual Jubilee night, many of the young ladies who had been been in the Guild dance competitions were seen even more of in cabarets at dinner-dances and at the Palais De Danse.

When the Guild and the Jubilee were over it was time to get ready for the visitors, and thanks to the beneficial effects of rearmament on pay-packets there were hopes of a good season. The following year there was a further royal distraction just as the final touches were being put on Guild test-pieces. There was a competition to chose the Isle of Man Beauty Queen, with real film stars as judges and the promise of a film test for the winner.

The Coronation Year of King Edward the Eighth was the occasion for the first performance of a cantata called *The Legend of Mann* at the Guild. It was conducted by its composer George Tootell, Doctor of Music, who had recently returned to become the organist at the new Regal Cinema. The soloists were adjudicator Stewart Robinson, Mr Buxton, and Nora Moore who was daughter of Noah Moore and was a former Baume Scholar. Kathleen Ryding handed over the leader's chair of the amateur orchestra to Felix Cohen, leader of the Liverpool Phil.

Astonishment, amusement and nostalgia

There was astonishment that Guild week when the youthful Edward Killen, who had never been heard in public until he had won his class three years earlier, won the Cleveland medal. The press said that his swift rise from obscurity had no parallels in the history of the festival, but it would appear that he did not sustain this early success. There was amusement when the dance adjudicator thought that the same little girl was trying to come back and perform again, as the audience knew that she was the second of the Calderbrook twins competing in turn. It was nostalgia time when Fred Minay Senior came out of musical retirement to sing in a quartet when

George Tootill and the Legend of Mann.

one of its members was taken ill, and that quartet included his son.

The old hands may also have reflected that they had heard it all before when they read in the *Isle of Man Examiner* the words of a new editor from Wales. He had discovered that the Manx were a musical nation.

"I heard choral singing that would set aflame the heart of every Welshman. Come Manxmen! when are you going to set up a choir to compete in the Welsh National Eisteddfod?"

He also claimed to have seen actors and actresses from a village in the north of the Island in a production that would have done credit to a London theatre, and he ended up with grandiosely naive proposals for "a Great Assembly, a

This photograph (by courtesy of Gladys Skillicorn) may evoke nostalgia.

National Festival of Arts and Crafts with the trappings of the Welsh Eisteddfod combined with a Great Homecoming and forming a major tourist attraction".

The thundering of Thor

In the spring of l939, the same paper drew attention to the fact that the male choir test piece, (Tootell's *Battle of Sandwat*) was about Thor, the god of war, and it urged the public to treat themselves to a respite from the thunderings of Thor by going to the Guild. The great victory of the week was for the choirs Douglas Buxton had taken over, as between them they won five trophies. There was a massed brass band concert conducted by adjudicator Fred Mortimer. There were 16 adult plays, together with six in the "under 18" class, and this was won by a Northern Ireland school which had entered two plays, one written by a schoolboy.

In the concert, Hadyn Wood conducted his choral work *Lochinvar*. The Cleveland winner was 22-year-old Bobby Nichol, and he was to sing his test piece in a broadcast. At the last moment the producer asked him to change the song, but when Bobby, who had hastily practised the new one, arrived to face the microphone, he was told to sing the original after all. Understandably, he had not brought its music, but fortunately somebody else had it with them.

An adjudicator that year fancied himself as a comedian and indulged in such one-liners as "the first duty of a pianist is to strike the right notes". However he did manage to strike the right note in respect of a test-piece which included the words "Though we have no arms to stack, we are perfect in our drill". He exclaimed that it sounded just like the territorial army, a unit of which had recently been raised in the Island.

After the 1939 festival was over, the thunderings of Thor were heard on the TT course, which was dominated by German riders on the motor bikes which were soon to be the scouts of the *blitzkrieg*.

A boost for the Baume Scholar

Another adjudicator raised an unintentional laugh when he said that it would be worth somebody giving a thorough musical education to the boy who won the ear-test. He was the son of Mr and Mrs T C Corris, both redoubtable music teachers and conductors, and his sister Alicia was the current Baume scholar.

For some years this scholarship had been insufficient for its purpose and had only been modestly augmented some ten years earlier out of a joint appeal by the World Manx Association and the Guild as a memorial to Florence Laughton. Then, for 1939, Elizabeth Cunningham of Holiday Camp fame donated £600 to the Baume Fund. In the 1920s she had combined her enthusiasm for Guiding with her musical talents and entered choirs for the Girl Guide class in the festival, often in competition with her daughter-in-law, Mrs Harley Cunningham, who was the first lady to win the Cleveland medal.

Paradoxically when the Baume Scholarship fell vacant in 1939 there was no applicant of suitable standard, so far as the Royal College of Music was concerned.

Top: *Douglas Buxton (middle row to right of shield) with the choir that won four trophies in 1939.*
Left: *A Douglas High School choir of the same era. (Photos courtesy of D Buxton)*

Keep the flag flying

The war was four months old in February 1940 when the Isle of Man Steam Packet Company announced excellent profits from the permanent charter of ships on war-service. Some people wondered how the visitors were going to get there in the coming summer, for after all it was then known as the "Phoney War". All the same, wartime restrictions on gold prevented the arrival of the Cleveland medal.

That year's Guild included a revived children's festival, announced as being with the whole-hearted cooperation of the teachers' association. The main concert was to include a cantata called *The Magic Isle* by the veteran J E Quayle, and the cellist in the amateur orchestra was a refugee from Nazi Germany. Unhappily an editorial protest declared that "He may be anti-Hitler, but we are not fighting Hitler, but the same Germany as last time", and the musician was forced to withdraw from the performance.

Before long, barbed wire had been put round blocks of boarding houses and there were many anti-Hitler musicians interned in the magic isle, while the next wave of visitors were fresh from the sands of Dunkirk. The £60 loss on the Guild was attributed to the blackout and parking restrictions on the promenade.

The following winter, night raids on big cities began, but it was all very remote from the Isle of Man, so that it was quite a shock when the Guild committee announced that, owing to uncertainly as to the future, there would be no Festival of Drama and Music in the spring. The press was critical of this defeatist attitude and riposted that

"while the flag of freedom was being hoisted in distant Bardia, the Guild committee were hauling down the flag of culture at home".

Then drama producer John Wrangham displayed the Dunkirk spirit by rallying the Manx Amateur Dramatic Federation to the flag, and urged it to put on a drama festival of its own. He made the reasonable request that the Guild committee should put up £50 to finance it, but less reasonably gave as his grounds that, while the drama box-office had kept the festival afloat, the amateur drama groups had always been £5 out of pocket on each entry, and the committee "was only interested in fostering singers who were supposed to be amateurs but got cash prizes if they won, and as a result sometimes received a guinea or two for a couple of songs at functions".

The resultant "drama-only" festival, which included a play called World Without Men with all-female cast, seemed to have been stronger on enthusiasm than organisation. Nobody brought along the trophies for the prize-giving and there was no pianist to play the national anthem. Nevertheless the event justifies the claim that the Manx Music Festival has run for 100 years without a break, even if there was no music that year.

In the meantime the considerable number of operational and training units of the armed forces stationed on the Island had been raising the flag of culture in all manner of entertainments. The extent to which they enlisted local talent, even to a concert in which three Cleveland medalists performed, and the success of frequent talent contests, suggests that the music side of the Guild could easily have been held.

The wartime festival

The first Wartime Festival of Music and Drama took place in 1942. As it was its silver jubilee year, special commemorative certificates were issued and Haydn Wood's specially composed *Ode to Genius* was to be performed; but publication problems caused its postponement until after the war. The normal rules were suspended, as was the award of prizes and trophies, and the competitions were opened up to service men and women stationed there, even if they were professional performers. Four such festivals took place, typically with 1,500 competitors, and the annual profits of up to £300 was given to war charities. As most other venues were in use by the armed forces, it was held in the Villa Marina.

The concerts, which were in the Gaiety Theatre, were on Sunday, and this upset some citizens as they did not have the predominantly "sacred" content customary for that day, but this did not seem to keep many people away. The committee said it could see no evil in holding it after church services, and it is to be hoped that the concern for wartime laxity of moral standards was assuaged by the re-introduction of a church organ competition.

For the first time ever, the concerts had the benefit of a professional concert orchestra. It was from the Royal Naval School of Music which was stationed on the Island, and its bandsmen, many of whom were boys, entered for a full range of specially created instrumental competitions and were a serious challenge to local young pianists and violinists. Dance band categories were introduced to utilise the talent from the two Royal Air Force airfields and elsewhere.

Many armed forces drama groups competed, often aided by local amateur actresses, and the Service Players, founded by naval officer Jon Pertwee of subsequent *Doctor Who* fame, became a permanent Manx dramatic society.

Faced with this influx, it is not surprising that when adult classes for recitation from the dialect works of T E Brown were re-introduced, there was minimal interest. However conventional elocution was popular, with such stirring pieces as *To Be or Not to Be* and *Give Me Liberty*. The printing in the programme of the nostalgic Manx ballad *Ellan Vannin* suggests that this was thought more appropriate than *O Land Of Our Birth* in the circumstances.

Participation by local young people was high, with 109 girls up to the age of 16 singing solos in 1945, and on one occasion an "under 16" choir was conducted by Wilfred Cowley who was also under 16. The adult singing competitions remained very much the domain of local people, although on one occasion two Leading Aircraftsmen from Jurby won a duet. Despite all this, one adjudicator commented "your lack of interest in music is a loss to this really worthwhile Guild", but this may have a back-handed compliment to the drama he was there to judge.

However when, by happy chance, Victory in Europe Day occurred during Guild week, the verdict of Stewart Robinson was more favourable. He declared: "On this historic night, one of the memories that will live with me is that I was listening to some exquisite singing by these girls." It may be inferred from this that the 25 mezzo-sopranos he had been judging were not

Douglas High School for Girls 1941 production of The Happy Man.

unduly distracted by the prospect of joy and laughter as soon as they got off the platform.

Peace ever after

The first peacetime festival reverted to the normal rules, and the trophies, which had been tarnishing in the vaults of the Isle of Man Bank, were brought out again. There were important changes in the committee. Treasurer Lewis Clague had died and been replaced by Town Clerk Percy Shimmin, who had been a successful soloist. George Tootell took over the secretary-ship from W A Craine.

Problems arose for the new secretary. Owing

to a double-booking, the high-capacity Palace Ballroom was not available for part of Guild Week, so it was arranged to spread out into the same company's Crescent Cinema and Pavilion together with the Coliseum and Gaiety Theatres. Then Blakemore's Music Shop announced that it was no longer able to handle the festival bookings. The Cleveland test got timetabled for 6pm which was not an ideal time for supporters who were at work.

A homecomer from Cleveland, Ohio came with both the new medal and the 1940 one, and found himself presenting them both to Dan Minay. When in the following year it went again to an existing winner, another such homecomer made remarks about having to save up dollars and dimes to pay for the medals, and the Cleveland Manx Society again requested in vain that it should not be awarded to anyone more than once.

The concert was very ambitious. It included a symphony by J E Quayle and the BBC Northern Orchestra with Charles Groves conducting was engaged at a cost of £300, as well as £62 for extra staging. This and the increased cost of hiring the various venues resulted in a loss of £150. There was some acrimony with the Palace and Derby Castle Company over the double-booking and the increase of charges since before the war, so it was decided to use the Villa Marina in future.

Ring down the curtain

At the time of the drama competitions in 1948, Field Marshal Lord Montgomery of Alamein was going to be on the Island. The local territorial regiment had been in his "Desert Rats" and he was to be honoured with the Freedom of the Borough of Douglas. It was also understood that Monty was going to present the drama prizes, but it transpired that he had not consented and he refused to oblige at short notice. A schoolboy at King William's College, the local public school, who played the part of an army officer in one of the plays was to follow Montgomery's footsteps into the Tank Corps and become a general. However he did end up giving out prizes at the Guild. His name was Laurence New, a recent Governor of the Isle of Man.

In 1948 drama had another contretemps. The committee had tried to economise in theatre bookings, only to find that there were not enough nights to put all the plays on, so it scheduled some for the afternoon. The drama federation protested that players could not turn up in the afternoon, so two more nights were booked. Then at the last moment some of the plays were scratched. Those extra nights had to be paid for, but largely due to the popularity of the plays there was an overall profit of £139 on that year's Guild.

The following year there were 27 one-act plays and the general view of them was still what the chairman, Speaker Qualtrough, had declared just before the war: "There is some talk of separating the drama festival from the Guild. Believe me, there is not the slightest possibility. The committee is very proud of the dramatic section, and if it should grow until it becomes even greater in number and importance than the music section, we shall wish it the greatest good luck."

Leighton Stowell (centre) with Folk Dance group 1947. (Photo courtesy of Doris Larsen)

The 1950 Guild was full of promise for the future, both in talent and numbers. There were 38 choral entries, 784 individual musical entries, 193 dance entries and 26 plays. Altogether some 3,000 individuals were involved. However as the 1950s advanced, tourism began to decline and there was a business recession and high unemployment. Younger people sought work elsewhere, and the next census revealed that during the 1950s the population had dropped by some 7,000 to 48,000, with an increased proportion of elderly people.

At the start of these lean years, it was taken for granted that the drama box-office would keep the Guild out of the red. Of course it had the odd storm in a teacup. The headmistress of Douglas High School suddenly decreed that her girls could no longer enter plays in the Guild, as they had done for years under teacher Kay Cowin. That very year her production of excerpts from George Tootill's operetta *Peggy and the Pixies* had been a great success.

The Head also announced that her pupils could not even spare time from their studies to take part in the 1951 Festival of Britain pageantry, as called for by the Governor, and so the Director of Education tried to resolve the problem. However his solution, which was that the Guild should be held in the Easter holidays, was rejected.

There was drama off the stage when it was discovered that the judge had added up the marks wrongly, so that St Mary's players should have been tied first instead of being a close second. He took the remarkable step of retrospectively awarding an extra mark to the Green Room Club, so that it would still be the winner.

Eliijah on stage around 1947. (Photo courtesy of Janice Percival)

After he had returned to London it was found that other marks were wrong so he made further amendments over the telephone.

It was about this time that the choirs pointed out that, unlike drama, they had no grant per entry, and even if they did win, their cash prize had not been increased since 1932, although the cost of music and hiring practice rooms had gone up considerably. Not to be outdone, the dramatic societies declared that their grant of £3 per play was likewise inadequate, and they asked for a laid-down scale of production expenses.

By 1956 the Manx Music and Drama Festival had a serious overdraft. It was cleared by selling investments, but the next year there was an even worse deficit. There were appeals to Tynwald for financial help, but it was not a time when there was any money to spare for such luxuries. The committee decided to eliminate events it judged to be uneconomical. Brass bands were dropped on the grounds that the number of entries no longer justified the expense of importing a special adjudicator. There had been allegations of falling standards in dance, and concern that some entries were accompanied by singing of a vulgar nature, and in 1958 all classes apart from country dancing were axed on the same grounds of expense. Unlike Brass, Dance was not revived in later years.

As the recent Opera and Lieder competitions, open to all pitches of voice with individual choice of song, had proved to have greater box-office appeal than classes where a succession of the same sort of voice sang the same test-piece, a new class for Light Opera was introduced on the same lines.

It was also realised that the traditional subscription system, which conferred a free programme and a season ticket, was a great bargain for the subscriber but was no longer making money for the festival. As these lean years were not the time to increase charges, the benefits were reduced.

However the main cause of loss was that the cost of the plays was exceeding their box-office takings. There was no shortage of drama entries, but the more plays there were, the more nights the theatre had to be hired, and there was a limit to the number of extra nights that drama supporters would buy tickets for. In 1956, the Gaiety Theatre cost £27.50 per night plus the wages of house and back-stage staff, while the rest of the festival was accommodated in the Villa Marina for £200 for the week, including staff. The plays received an entry subsidy, while other classes paid entry fees.

In the hope of getting through more plays per night, the drama federation was asked to provide a stage organiser. Then in 1959, half of the £240 loss was attributable to drama. It was proposed to economise by hiring the Villa Marina concert hall for two days only and scattering the displaced events around various church halls, which was likely to discourage attendance and alienate music from drama. The committee had evolved to meet the needs of a festival which had no drama, and the drama groups looked to their own federation for aspirations which their representatives on the Guild committee would raise.

Finally in 1960, when the loss on the plays approximated to the entire overdraft, the Guild

Opposite: 1948 winning production by Kay Cowin of scene from Midsummer Night's Dream.

Above: Dancing fairies from Ramsey 1952.

Right: 1952 winners: Dance Duet Vicki Moorhouse and Sandra Clayton (back) and National Dance soloist Susan Kelly. (Dance photos by courtesy of Mrs C E Conway)

chairman and secretary proposed to their committee to discontinue drama. It was not carried, but at the subsequent AGM there was surprise and relief when Mr Lynch, secretary of the drama federation, announced that his committee had decided, only the previous night, to bring down the curtain.

It was amicably agreed that the federation should secede without any liability for the losses attributable to the plays, and the donors of the drama trophies were asked to agree to their use in the one-act play festival they proposed to run on their own. Unfortunately this did not survive for long, but the various elocution and dramatic competitions remained as part of the Music Festival festival and flourished.

Leider finals in 1953 with Rev F Cubbon donor of trophy in centre, and Douglas Quirk, Gladys Skillicorn, Charles Hindley, Eileen Peters (winner), and Jack Gelling (Photo by courtesy of Gladys Skillicorn)

In l960 the Legion Players were winners of the last drama competition. Ironically the play was called "A Musical Evening". (Photo courtesy of Rene Savage)

Chapter 4

1961-1991:
Modern times

The l961 Manx Music Festival eliminated the debt which stood at about £500. There had been some fund-raising and certain choirs had made the gesture of returning their previous year's prize money, but the beneficial change was to abandon the concert which involved the engagement of professional soloists. The big night became the one on which the Cleveland test and other major competitions were held, and subscribers had to pay for this event.

The following year's Cleveland test was notable for the fact that there were no previous medalists in it, and that Kathleen Cooil was the first contralto ever to win. Five years earlier Robert Kendrick, who had made his Guild debut in 1952, became the first person from outside the Island to win the Cleveland medal.

Meanwhile however, there was no shortage of "special class" singers and Cleveland finalists who were from local families which had been long involved in the Guild. In 1954, the year Mr Kendrick first reached the Cleveland test, the press emphasised this by commenting on the creditable performance of three sisters with the names of Crowe, Gelling and Fargher, and noted that five other close relatives had also been competing.

Likewise, when reporting on the successes of Margaret Curphey, the 1960 Cleveland medalist who was to have a eminent professional singing career, they stressed her membership of a singing family of Curpheys and Gellings. They did the same in 1966 when Phillip Gelling, who also became a successful professional singer, reached and won the Cleveland in competition with some of his own musical clan.

In 1953 Harry Pickard, the brother of three creditable singing sisters, added a new dimension to Manx choral life when he took his choir on an overseas tour, something he had tasted when running a choir in the Manx Regiment. He became the Island's first schools music teacher/adviser, a post now held by his son Allan.

Needless to say, the perennial belief that the young were not perpetuating their musical heritage was advanced in 1959 as the reason for the impending financial collapse of the Guild, when a paper asserted that it was "suffering from the changing habits and in particular the changing educational system which no longer provides the foundation on which the Guild was built — the children!". Nevertheless two thirds of the entries in 1961 were from children and teenagers.

As the swinging Sixties unfolded, grants for higher education and good employment opportunities elsewhere were taking away young people who in harder times would would have been continuing to apply their talents to the Guild. The new permissiveness was not conducive to teenagers staying at home and practising the "songs my mother taught me", while anyone who thought they had mastered the three chord trick could do their own thing in the new music of youth culture. The only concession to their interests was a new class for the electronic organ and, in 1970, for folk-singing with guitar. It is all the more remarkable therefore, that in one year in the mid-Sixties there were 510 "under-16" entries, including 173 girl soloists.

Meanwhile the Manx tax haven policy of the 1960s was attracting displaced empire builders as the winds of change blew though the Commonwealth and in 1966 the committee was asked to contact these new residents with a view to their becoming subscribers. Such people would have found the conversation at that year's festival intriguing.

Quite apart from reciting the musical genealogies of the performers of whom the adjudicator said that the Island had more out-standing singers to the square mile than any other part of the British Isles, the natives may have got rather restless when the prizes were handed out by a distinguished representative of the British Government instead of the customary Governor or his deputising deemster.

Soon after, these newcomers would be further reminded that the Isle of Man was different by the singing of the Manx national anthem without *God Save the Queen*, and by the new class in reading from the Manx bible. However they could take solace in another new competition for songs by British composers.

The Sixties were also a time when the world was said to be turning into an electronic village, although when in 1965 the first broadcasts from the Guild went out on Manx Radio, not many Manx villages could pick them up. However, the Guild was heard in Cleveland, Ohio and other World Manx strongholds, as audiotapes were sent out. Two years later Border Television made a broadcast from the Guild featuring the Cleve-land winner, Mrs Eleanor Shimmin.

Then a BBC *Friday Night Is Music Night* took place, and a choir of 200 was mustered. It sang the recent Guild 50-voice test piece. There was little evidence that choral enthusiasm was declin-ing apart from the fact that few church choirs were competing other than Emily Christian's one from Rosemount (Trinity).

However some of this enthusiasm was being diverted into ambitious concerts of the sort which had ceased to be a feature of the Manx Music Festival. Some were enhanced by the importation of professional soloists with financial help from the new Isle of Man Arts Council. Its spokesman was Cecil McFee, who was a member of Tynwald and a conductor of Guild choirs. He had some novel ideas to stimulate interest in the Guild. At one extreme he proposed that a number of village eisteddfods be set up, with the winners offered free entry in the Guild. At the other he proposed that there be a special adjudi-cator for the Cleveland test who would also give a celebrity concert.

In 1970, Guild Week expanded to occupy seven days. Karen Vaughan became the first harpist to win the Baume Scholarship, and a new literature-writing class attracted 29 entries. The next census revealed that the Island's population had increased by 8,000 in the Sixties.

Looking back and looking forward

In the last 20 years, the way of life out of which the Manx Music Festival arose has finally changed out of all recognition. The finance sector has overtaken tourism as the main occupation, so that music-making is no longer "something to do in the winter". For the consequent newcomers the Manx Musical Festival, although not part of their family history, is an event where they and their children can find common ground with an important feature of the Manx way of life.

With the extensive provision of musical education and of concerts, the Guild is no longer the sole "centre of musical work and interest" but it is still a unique and major stimulus for performers, young and old. Concessions to changing taste include a small-group class called *Music For Fun*, introduced in 1988. The choice of music may be Pop, and part of the fun can be a pun on the producer's name, like *Gale Force* and *Corrin's Follies*. In contrast, the new class in 1991 for Victorian and Edwardian Ballads has already demonstrated that composers such as Haydn Wood have lost none of their appeal.

Since 1979 those who wish to perpetuate the memory of someone who was involved in the Guild have been encouraged to give to a Special Prize Fund to be used for a particular purpose each year, rather than add to the plethora of prizes and trophies dedicated to particular events. Since 1986, there have been workshops run by the adjudicators at the end of the festival, and they have been for brass, strings, speech and singers between the ages of 16 and 25.

Some of the historic trophies have became redundant reminders of the decline of competitive choral singing. In 1991, there were only four ladies choirs and one male-voice choir. However there were 44 "under 18" choral entries. Other 1991 comparisons between young and old are approximately as follows, quartets being counted as four entries:

Above and opposite: Two people who were involved in many ways with the Guild have been honoured for their services to music. Miss Emily Christian seen here with choral trophies, was awarded the MBE (Photo courtesy of Mrs and Mrs G Christian). Douglas Buxton, pictured with the Lhon Vane Choir, was made a Freeman of the Borough of Douglas.

Voice	Under 18: 240	Over 18: 530
Piano	Under 16: 90	Over 18: 30
Recorder	Under 16: 90	No over 18 class
Other instruments	Under 16: 75	Over 16: 40

Brass instruments were popular with all ages, with 13 brass quartet entries and 18 ensembles or bands.

Since few appraising remarks have been made by the press in the past 20 years, the views were sought of a few people who have been involved with the Guild in a wide range of capacities for a long time.

There were comments that there are still plenty of good young voices coming up, and there is good musical education in schools, but it is instrumental, not vocal, and that there is a shortage of voice-production specialists. The view was advanced that choirs which undertake concert tours abroad do less for the Island's listening public than they did in the past, when the best choirs used to perform in every church, chapel and hall.

As regards the major competitions, it was

conjectured that if there were no Cleveland test, there might be a desire to regard the winner of what was regarded as the most demanding competition for all voice-compasses, such as oratorio, as the Island's best singer. It was also pointed out that singers now compete, who while not professional performers, have been to music conservatoires, so that comparisons are no longer just between those with local training.

In recent years, the various speech classes have attracted an average of 350 entrants , mostly young people. People who had been involved in the pre-1960 drama competitions recalled that such classes had once been more drama-oriented.

Cleveland Medallists rehearsing for a concert to raise funds for the Centenary. (Photo courtesy of Barbara Gale)

It was pointed out that while the festival does have a class for "Songs From the Musicals" it has none in which singers are required to show that they can also act or dance. Yet these skills are in increasing demand to a high standard in local amateur productions and are frequently required of singers attending music colleges.

For the past 14 years the revived Chruinnaght has been the focal gathering for Pan-Celtic folk culture. Before that the Manx Music Festival was the major means by which this culture was re-kindled in each generation, and its competitions still stimulate its cultivation in schoolchildren. The view of someone who has been involved in both movements for many years was that, in contrast with spontaneous and sociable perform-ance, formal competition is a constraint on the development of folk music.

The Baume Scholarship is now at the disposal of the Education Department, available to give a little help to anyone not eligible for a state grant, but it is apparently unused. The new equivalent is the Bank of Ireland Young Musician of Mann Competition, open to those who are successful in the instrumental classes of the Manx Music Festival.

One common recollection which was related, even by people who have risen to the top in public life, was of the shock of being pushed out at a tender age to sing or play on the platform of a huge and cold auditorium. Facing the public in this way may have prepared them for later life, but with less compulsion and competition in schooling of late, it must be an even greater shock for some of today's children. However current trends in education may bring about a swing of the pendulum, and it remains to be seen whether the National Curriculum will nurture music and national culture.

It goes without saying that the future of the Manx Music Festival depends on the young, and many of the young competitors of the 1960s are now the parents and teachers who are passing on the musical foundation their families gave them,

A Cleveland Winner receives the medal.

so that in the 1992 Manx Music Festival there will be entrants who are the great-great grandchildren — if not even greater — of those who stood up in the first Music Guild a century ago.

But whatever the future brings, the highlights of its past will surely be remembered with pride — and perhaps with prejudice — wherever people sing:

"Then let us rejoice
With heart, soul and voice."

Young and old players in Ramsey Town Band in the 1970s.

Children from St John's School who competed in Manx language classes in 1976.

Also from Leading Edge

Mann Ablaze!
A history of the Isle of Man Fire Service
by Stan Basnett

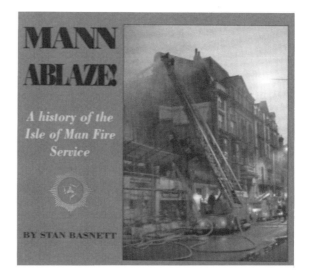

A comprehensive and fully illustrated history of fire fighting in the Isle of Man charting the early incidence of life
threatening fire, the development of the various brigades
and creation in 1965 of a fire service covering the whole
island.

Stan Basnett is a Manxman by birth and lifelong island
resident. He is also the principal author of the successful
The Isle of Man by Tram, Train and Foot, published by
Leading Edge in its RailTrail series.

ISBN 0 948135 25 5   £6.75

*'A fascinating book....worth buying for the illustrations
alone'* Manx Tales
'A splendid documentary' Manx Independent

Forthcoming titles ...

Hidden Places of Mann – *also by Stan Basnett*   ISBN 0 948135 39 5
A sequel to *The Isle of Man by Tram, Train and Foot*

100 years of the Manx Electric Railway *by Keith Pearson*
A revised and updated version of *Isle of Man Tramways*, the "bible" of the Manx electric railway system.
ISBN 0 948135 38 7